# Giant Sticker Activity BOYS

MiLeS KeLLy

First published in 2009 by Miles Kelly Publishing Ltd
Bardfield Centre, Great Bardfield, Essex CM7 4SL

This edition printed in 2009

2 4 6 8 10 9 7 5 3

**Editorial Director:** Belinda Gallagher
**Art Director:** Jo Brewer
**Assistant Editor:** Carly Blake
**Volume Designers:** Carmen Johnson, Joe Jones
**Cover Designer:** Simon Lee
**Image Manager:** Lorraine King
**Production Manager:** Elizabeth Brunwin
**Reprographics:** Ian Paulyn

ISBN 978-1-84810-121-0

Printed in China

British Library Cataloguing-in-Publication Data
A catalogue record for this book is available from the British Library

ACKNOWLEDGEMENTS
All artworks from the Miles Kelly Artwork Bank

The publishers would like to thank the following sources
for the use of their photographs:
Page 36 Hyakutake comet Andrew Kazmierski/Fotolia.com; 60 vintage camera Stephen Coburn/Fotolia.com,
polaroid camera Vasyl Dudenko/Fotolia.com; 61 trainers amridesign/Fotolia.com, television Kwest/Fotolia.com,
fridge Kirsty Pargeter/Fotolia.com, laptop Fatman73/Fotolia.com, games console photazz/Fotolia.com;
69(t) Walt Disney/Pictorial Press, (cr) W.Disney/Everett/Rex Features

All other photographs are from:
Corel, digitalSTOCK, digitalvision, iStockphoto.com, John Foxx, PhotoAlto,
PhotoDisc, PhotoEssentials, PhotoPro, Stockbyte

Made with paper from a sustainable forest

www.mileskelly.net
info@mileskelly.net

www.factsforprojects.com
The one-stop homework helper — pictures, facts, videos, projects and more

# DEADLY CREATURES

# Deadly Creatures

Grey wolf

Many animals have to fight to survive. Some kill for food — these animals are called predators.

Others only kill to defend themselves, their young or their homes.

Whatever the reason for using their claws, jaws or venom, these creatures are fascinating but deadly!

► Wolves show their teeth and growl when they are angry. This is called snarling.

# Here are some other deadly creatures...

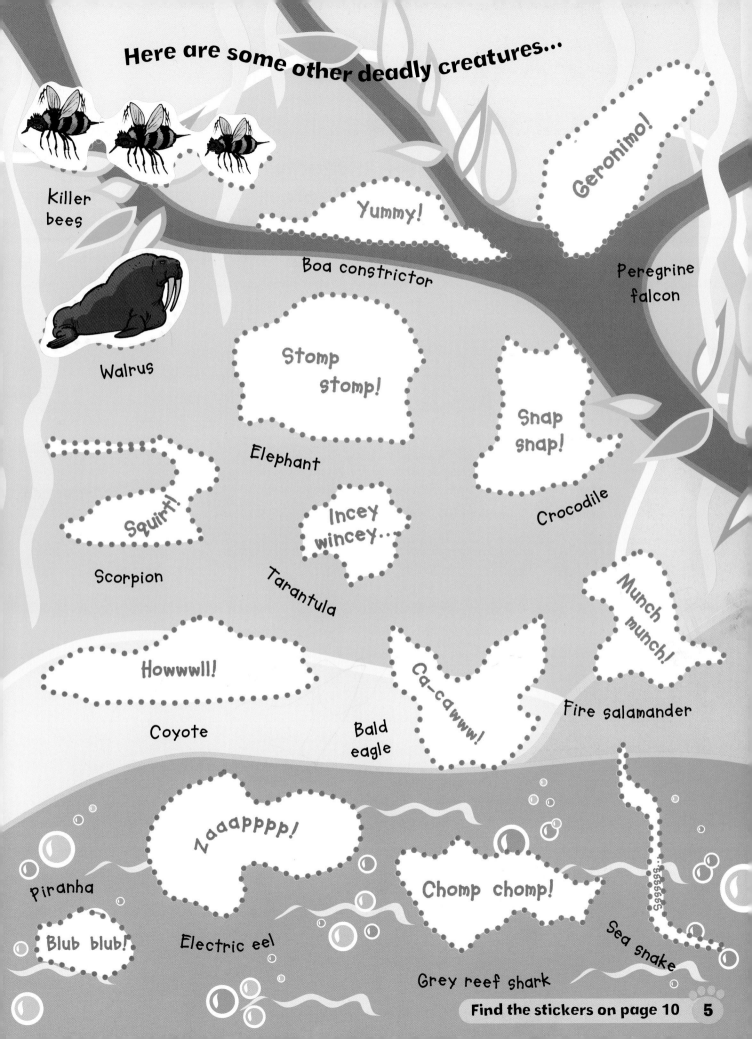

Killer bees

Walrus

Yummy!

Boa constrictor

Geronimo!

Peregrine falcon

Stomp stomp!

Elephant

Snap snap!

Crocodile

Squirt!

Scorpion

Incey wincey...

Tarantula

Munch munch!

Fire salamander

Howwwll!

Coyote

Ca-cawww!

Bald eagle

Zaaapppp!

Piranha

Chomp chomp!

Blub blub!

Electric eel

Sea snake

Grey reef shark

**Find the stickers on page 10**  **5**

# Crocodiles and alligators

**Lurking beneath the water, a deadly hunter waits! Crocodiles and alligators spend most of their time in water. They are the biggest reptiles on Earth.**

Crocodiles have their top and bottom teeth showing when their jaws are shut, but alligators only have their top teeth showing.

Crocodiles have huge jaws full of teeth. They use their teeth for grabbing and biting their prey.

Crocodile

Like crocodiles, alligators are strong reptiles with wide jaws and thick, scaly skin.

Alligator

## Hunting

A crocodile lies very still in the water until an animal comes close. Then it attacks! When the crocodile has the animal in its jaws, it pulls it under water and spins it around.

# Food

Crocodiles and alligators will eat anything that comes close enough to bite! This includes turtles, snakes, monkeys, cows and pigs... Sometimes even humans!

Crocodile

Feed the hungry croc!

Yum!

Yum!

Yum!

## 'Gator gallery!

American alligator

Dwarf crocodile

Saltwater crocodile

Chinese alligator

Gharial

Mugger

Black caiman

**Find the stickers on page 12**

# Birds of prey

Eagles, hawks, falcons, owls and ospreys are super predators called birds of prey.

Eagle owl

The eagle owl is so big and strong that it hunts other owls to eat.

Tawny owl

## Talons

Birds of prey have long, sharp claws called talons, which help them to catch animals to eat.

Talons

# Bird gallery!

Golden eagle

Tawny owl

Sparrow hawk

Osprey

African fish eagle

Red-tailed hawk

Bald eagle

## DOT-TO-DOT AND COLOUR

...this bald eagle! Bald eagles live on a diet of fish that they swipe out of the water using their talons.

**Use these stickers on page 5**

**Stickers for fun – use anywhere you like**

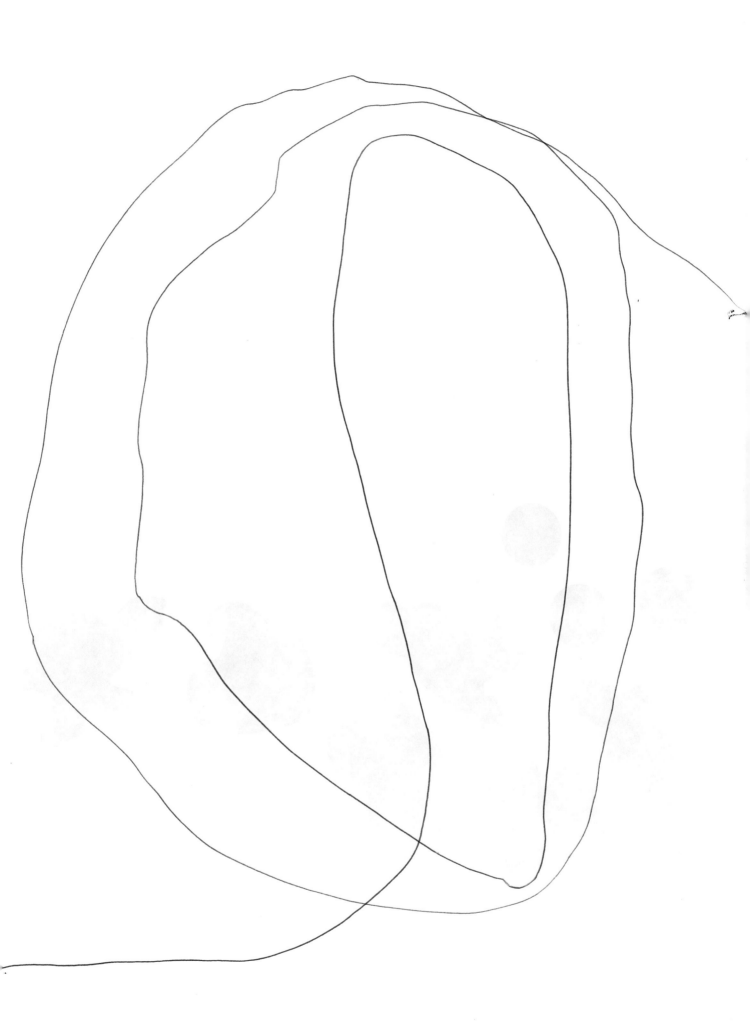

**Use these stickers on pages 6, 7, 8 and 17**

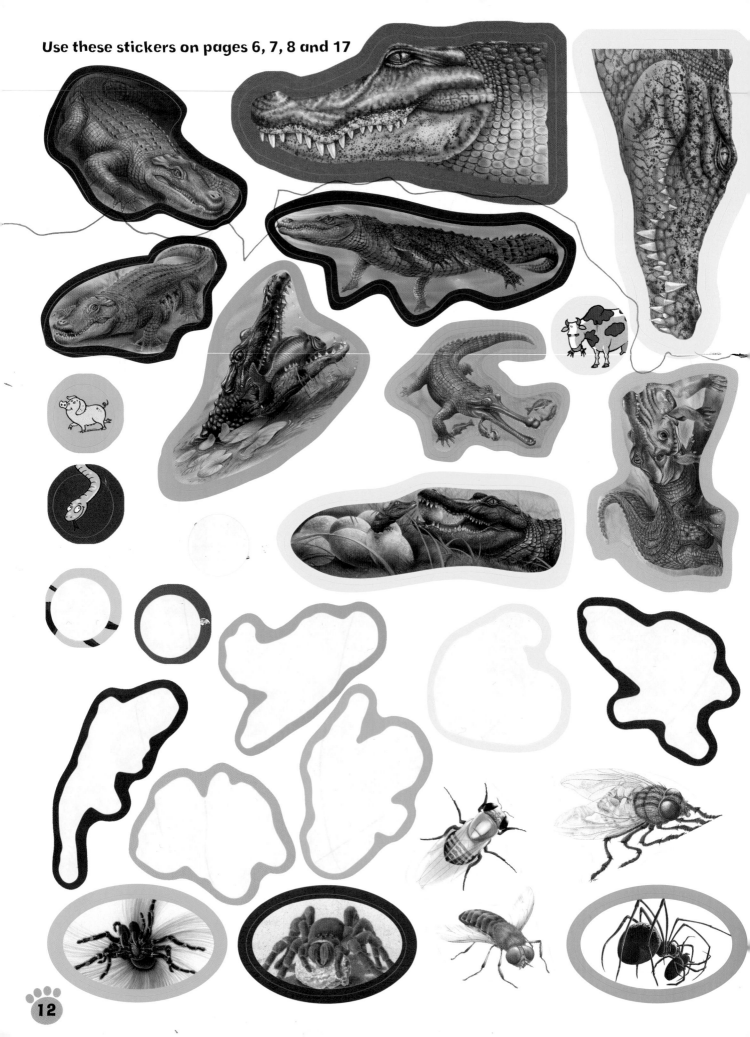

Use these stickers on pages 18, 19 and 20

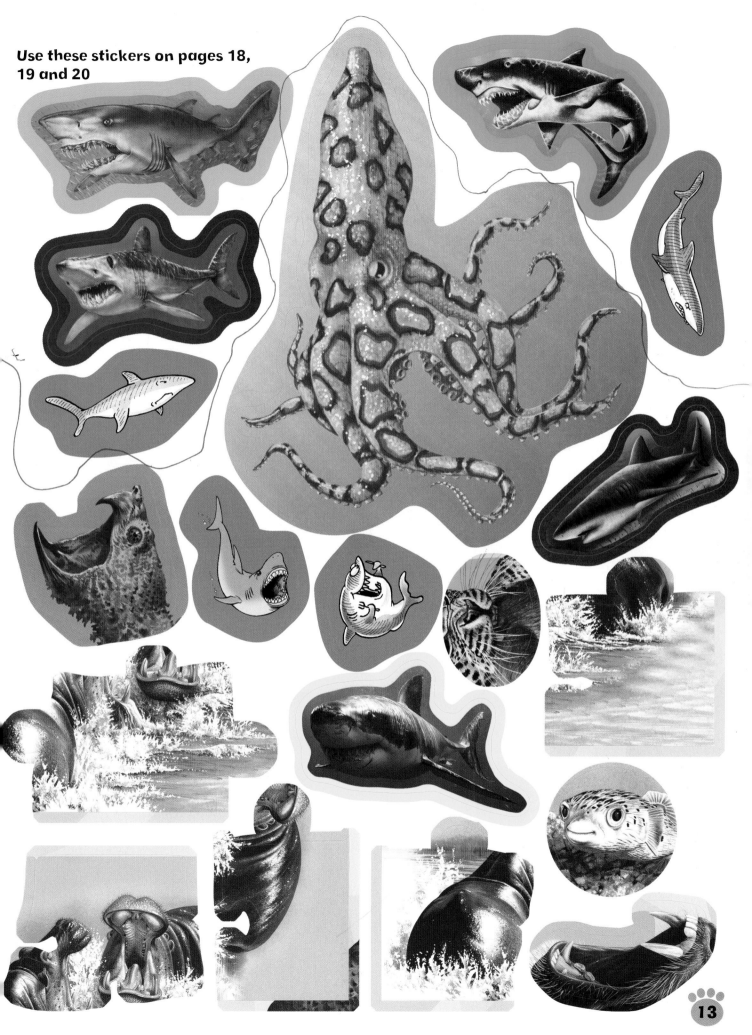

13

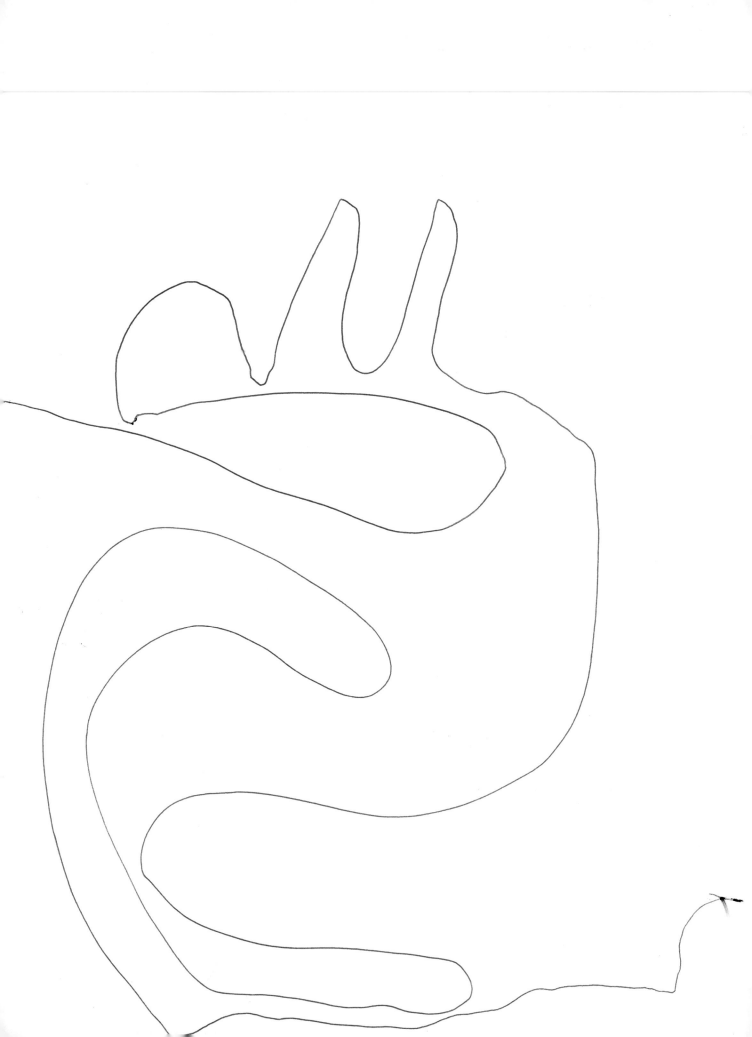

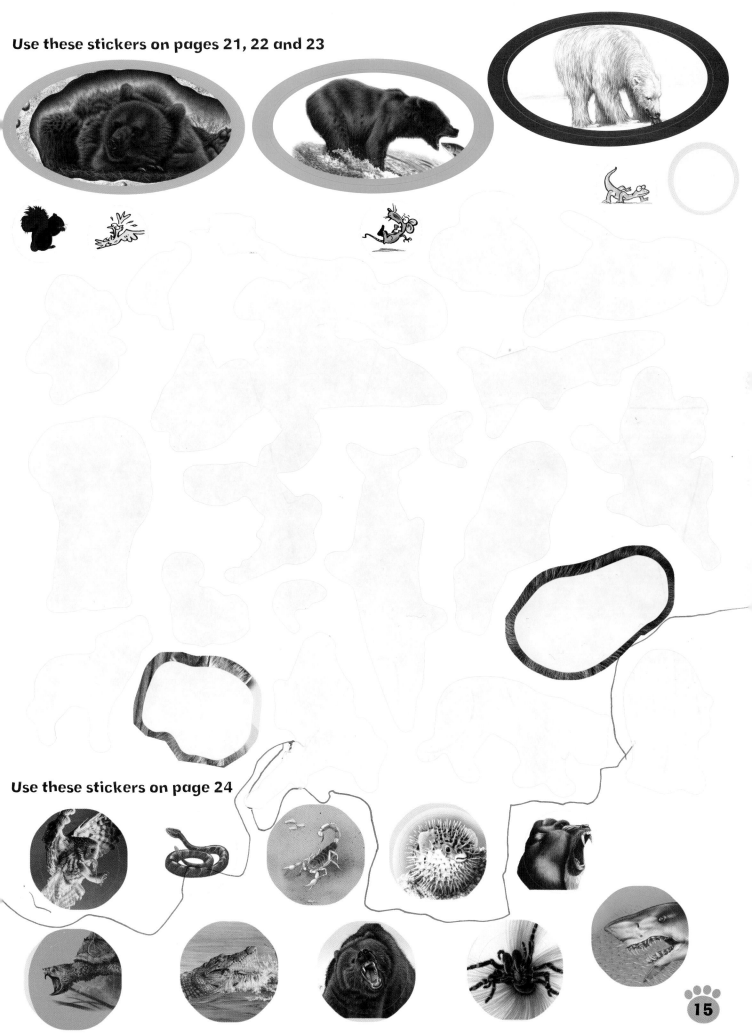

**Use these stickers on pages 21, 22 and 23**

**Use these stickers on page 24**

15

# Bugs

Some bugs have fangs or stings that can inject a deadly poison called venom into their prey. Others bugs carry deadly diseases that are harmful to humans.

Death stalker scorpions grab their prey in their pincers and sting it, injecting a deadly poison.

Death stalker scorpion

## Stings

Wasp

Bee

Hornets, wasps and bees have stings in their tails that inject a small amount of venom. Stings cause swelling and pain.

Hornet

## Bites

Mosquitoes are among the deadliest creatures. They can spread harmful diseases such as malaria when they bite people.

Mosquito

## Spider corner

These eight-legged creatures are types of bugs called arachnids (a-rak-nids). All spiders can bite and inject venom, but only around 200 species are harmful to humans.

Tarantula

Black widow

Funnel web spider

Horsefly

Buzz...

What is caught in the web?

Buzz...

Fruit fly

House fly

Buzz...

**Find the stickers on page 12**

# Into the water

Deep in oceans and rivers lurk some of the deadliest creatures in the world. There are sharp-toothed hunters, venomous stingers and spiny killers.

Red piranha

## Teeth

Red piranhas live in the Amazon river in South America. Their long, razor-sharp teeth make them scary-looking fish. They work together to attack prey such as birds.

Blue-ringed octopus

One sting from the blue-ringed octopus has enough venom to kill ten people.

ACTUAL SIZE!

## Venom

The most dangerous octopus in the world measures just 10 to 20 centimetres in length. The blue-ringed octopus grabs its prey with its tentacles before biting it.

Cone shell

Cone shells hunt other snails and fish. To kill its prey, the cone shell shoots a poisonous dart into the animal.

18

# Spikes

Some animals defend themselves. The spiny puffer fish swallows water to puff out its body and make its spines stand on end. The stonefish uses its spines to inject a deadly venom.

Spiny puffer fish

After

Before

Stonefish

# Hunters

Sharks are fish and most of them are hunters. The world's biggest hunting shark is the great white. It is 6 metres long and weighs more than one tonne!

Chomp!

Snap!

Chomp!

Snap!

What is chasing this diver?

# Shark gallery!

Tiger shark

Shortfin mako shark

Great white shark

Bull shark

Sand tiger shark

**Find the stickers on page 13**

# Fearsome bites

**Many deadly creatures can give a fearsome bite! Some have long, dagger-like teeth called fangs. Others have sharp, snapping beaks.**

Mandrill

Leopards have strong, sharp teeth that are good for holding onto prey. These big cats drag their food up into trees to eat it.

A mandrill's fangs can grow to 7 centimetres in length!

Mandrills are primates like monkeys. Male mandrills show their fangs to scare other males, or if they are scared.

Leopard

Put the right mouths on the animals!

Alligator snapping turtle

Instead of teeth or fangs, the alligator snapping turtle has a sharp beak. It snaps up fish, crabs and even other turtles!

# Picture Puzzle

Male hippos use their massive teeth as weapons to fight one another.

Rattlesnake

# Snacks

Venomous snakes, such as the rattlesnake, have large fangs. Rattlesnakes usually eat squirrels, mice, rabbits, lizards and birds.

Feed me!

Feed me!

Feed me!

Feed me!

Feed me!

## Feed the hungry snake!

False vampire bat

# Bone crushing

False vampire bats have sharp teeth. They catch and feed on frogs, mice, birds, and other bats. They kill their prey by biting its head and crushing its skull.

# Bear corner

Bears roar and bare their teeth to defend themselves. Most bears eat fish and plants, but the polar bear eats seals. The Kodiak bear is the biggest bear and lives in Alaska.

Kodiak bear

Polar bear

Eurasion brown bear

Brown bear

**Find the stickers on pages 13 and 15**

# Can you find...?

Chomp! ...A huge, scaly reptile with big teeth

A bird of prey with a sharp beak and claws... Hooo!

Whip! ...A scary scorpion with a sting in its tail

A deadly, eight-legged creature... Eek!

Blub! ...A fish that looks like a spiky ball

A terrifying hunting shark... Snap!

Ooh ooh! ...A frightening primate with very long teeth

A poisonous snake with a rattle in its tail... Ssss!

Crunch! ...A snappy turtle with a deadly bite

A huge, fearsome bear... Grrr!

# SPACE

# All about...

## Space

Astronaut

Here on Earth's surface you are surrounded by air. If you go upwards, up a mountain or in an aircraft, the air becomes thinner until there is none at all. This is where space begins.

It is impossible to imagine how big space is but there are many exciting things out there such as planets, stars and galaxies!

▶ Astronauts wear special space suits. They hold air for the astronauts to breathe and protect them from the Sun's heat.

# Here are some other space objects...

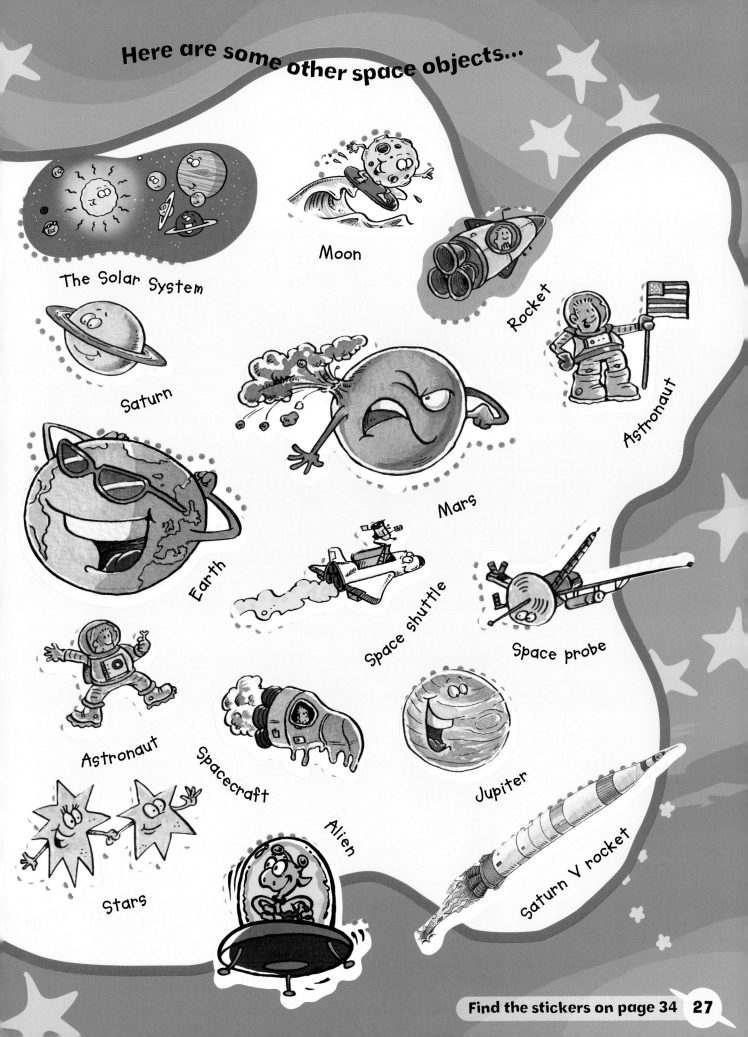

The Solar System

Moon

Rocket

Astronaut

Saturn

Mars

Earth

Space shuttle

Space probe

Astronaut

Spacecraft

Jupiter

Stars

Alien

Saturn V rocket

Find the stickers on page 34

# The Solar System

Sun

Mercury

Earth

Saturn

Jupiter

Venus

Mars

**The Sun and its eight circling planets make up the Solar System. Mercury is nearest the Sun, followed by Venus, Earth, Mars, Jupiter, Saturn, Uranus and Neptune.**

Stick in the missing labels!

# Earth and its neighbours

The planet we live on is Earth and Venus and Mars are the nearest planets to it. Venus is closer to the Sun than Earth, while Mars is farther away.

Venus is the hottest planet. It is hotter than Mercury, even though Mercury is closer to the Sun. Venus is covered by clouds that trap the Sun's heat.

Mars has the largest volcano in the Solar System. It is three times as high as Mount Everest, the tallest mountain on Earth.

Earth

Mars

Venus

28

# Biggest of all

Jupiter is the biggest planet – bigger than all the other planets in the Solar System put together! It is still much smaller than the Sun.

**Jupiter is 11 times wider than the Earth!**

Jupiter

# Smallest of all

Mercury is the smallest planet – it is a little larger than the Moon. Being the nearest planet to the Sun, temperatures can get twice as hot as an oven.

Uranus

Neptune

Mercury

# Planet gallery!

Earth

Saturn

Uranus

Mars

Mercury

Jupiter

Venus

Neptune

# How many?

Count how many of each item there are on these pages and write your answers in the boxes.

| Astronaut | Sun | Jupiter | Mercury | Comet | Earth | Rocket | Uranus |
|-----------|-----|---------|---------|-------|-------|--------|--------|
| 6 | 7 | 3 | 4 | 6 | 2 | 8 | 2 |

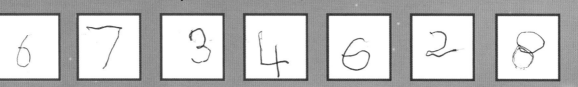
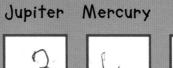

# The Moon

There are many moons in the Solar System and all of them travel around planets. The Earth has one moon, but other planets have more.

# Changing Moon

The Moon circles the Earth. Because it reflects light from the Sun, we see it shining. The Moon appears to change shape because we only see the part that is lit by the Sun, but it is always round.

## Moon gallery!

New Moon

Full Moon

Crescent Moon

First quarter Moon

Gibbous Moon

## DOT-TO-DOT AND COLOUR

...this lunar module. The lunar module is the part of the spacecraft that took astronauts to land on the surface of the Moon.

**Use these stickers on page 27**

**Stickers for fun – use anywhere you like**

**Use these stickers on pages 28 and 29**

**Use these stickers on pages 32 and 41**

**Use these stickers on pages 42 and 43**

36

**Use these stickers on page 43**

**Use these stickers on pages 44 and 45**

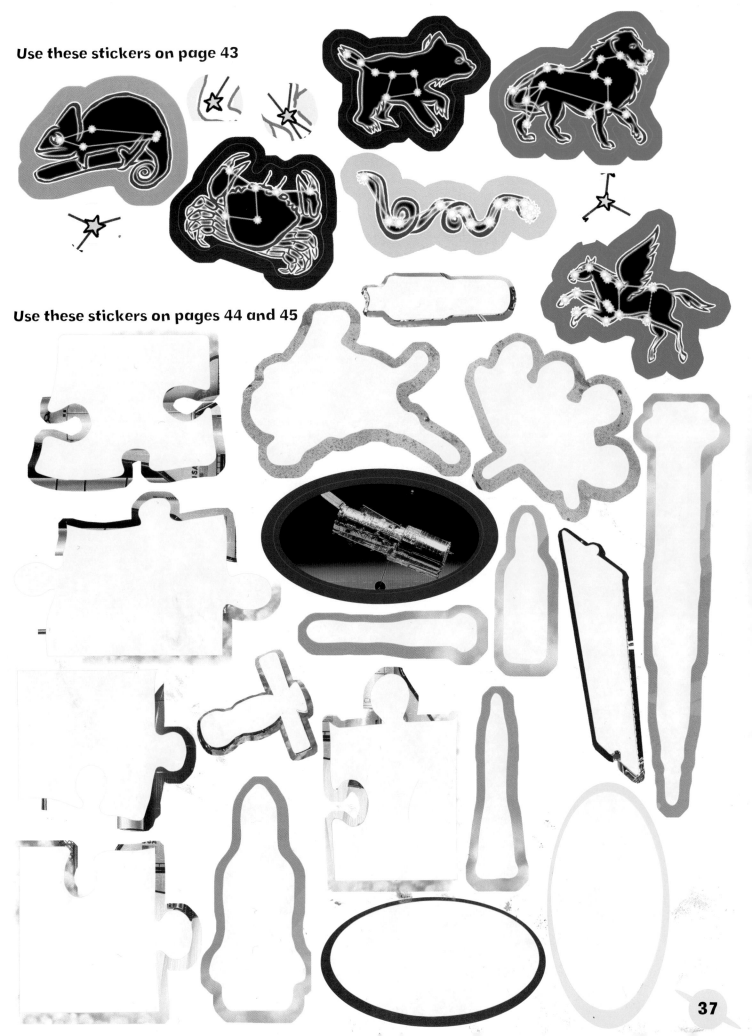

Use these
stickers on
page 48

# Space rocks

**Meteors, asteroids and comets are chunks of rock in space. Meteors are smaller rocks that have broken off asteroids. They can be as small as a pebble or as big as a car. Asteroids are made out of dust, rock and iron and can be as big as a house!**

If meteors enter the Earth's atmosphere, they burn up and make glowing streaks in the sky. These are called shooting stars.

Shooting stars

Jupiter

Mars

Asteroids are chunks of rock that failed to stick together to make a planet. Lots of them circle the Sun between Mars and Jupiter.

Asteroid belt

# Comet corner

Comets are made of rock, dust and ice. Heat from the Sun melts the ice and this makes dust and gas stream away from the comet. This forms a long, glowing tail.

What can the girl see?

Hale-bopp comet

Hyakutake comet

Halley's comet

Find the stickers on page 36 **41**

# Stars

Stars are super-hot balls of gas. You can see them glowing in the sky on a clear night. A star begins life in a giant cloud of dust and gas called a nebula.

New star

Nebula

Cluster of young stars

## Young stars

Young stars often form groups called clusters. Over time the stars slowly drift apart.

The centre of a star is very hot. It can be up to 16 million°C.

Large white star

## Types of star

Large stars are very hot and white. Smaller stars are cooler and redder and shine less brightly. Medium-sized stars are yellow like the Sun.

Medium-sized star

Small red star

# Galaxies

The Sun is part of a family of stars called the Milky Way galaxy. There are billions of stars in the Milky Way – as many as the grains of sand on a beach. Galaxies come in different shapes – the Milky Way is a spiral galaxy.

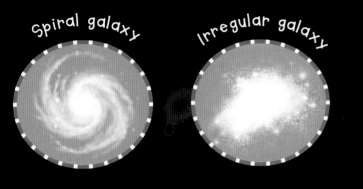

Spiral galaxy    Irregular galaxy    Elliptical galaxy    Barred spiral galaxy

# Constellations

A constellation is a pattern of stars. Many have been named after the shapes they seem to make. Different constellations are seen in different parts of the world.

Complete the constellation!

Ursa Major 'Great Bear'

# Constellation gallery!

Pegasus

Cancer

Ursa Minor 'Little Bear'

Hydra

Chameleon

Leo

# People in space

A space station is a place for astronauts to live in space. It has areas to sleep and eat, and even toilets! The longest time an astronaut has lived on a space station is just over a year.

The International Space Station is built up from parts that fit together like a jigsaw.

## Space shuttle

The space shuttle can carry up to eight astronauts into space and stay in orbit for ten days. The shuttle also takes parts into space to help build the International Space Station.

Cargo bay

Flight deck

Crew quarters

## Picture puzzle

The space shuttle is blasted into space by two giant rocket boosters.

# Rocket power

Rockets are used to launch spacecraft into space. A rocket needs enough fuel and power to reach great speeds of 40,000 kilometres an hour. If it moves any slower it will not be able to travel out of the Earth's atmosphere.

*Find the rockets!*

The rocket Saturn V launched the Apollo 11 Moon mission into space. The astronauts on board took the first ever steps on the Moon.

Titan    Ariane    Vostok    Energiya launcher/Buran spacecraft    Saturn V

# Explorer corner

Scientists use telescopes and robot spacecraft called probes to explore and take photos of the planets in our Solar System. The Viking probes landed on Mars in 1976 to explore the surface. The Sojourner rover explored Mars in 1997.

Sojourner rover

Voyager 2 probe

*Find the Mars explorers!*

Viking lander

Hubble Space Telescope

Galileo probe

**Find the stickers on page 39**

# Can you find...?

Wow! ...The biggest planet in our Solar System

The smallest planet in our Solar System... Aaah!

Stomp! ...A footprint left on the Moon.

A shower of shooting stars... Whoosh!

Phew! ...A kind of star that is like our Sun

A type of galaxy that is spiral shaped... Weee!

Snap! ...The constellation that looks like a crab

A spacecraft that flies astronauts into space... Zoom!

Roaarr! ...The rocket that launched Apollo 11

A robot explorer that landed on Mars... Bump!

# INVENTIONS

# Inventions

Light bulb

People have been inventing for thousands of years.

Our ancient relatives began inventing more than 400,000 years ago by making stone tools.

Science and modern technology has now filled our lives with machines and gadgets that have changed the way we live.

← American Thomas Edison invented the air-tight light bulb in 1879. Previous bulbs failed because air could get in, which made them burn out.

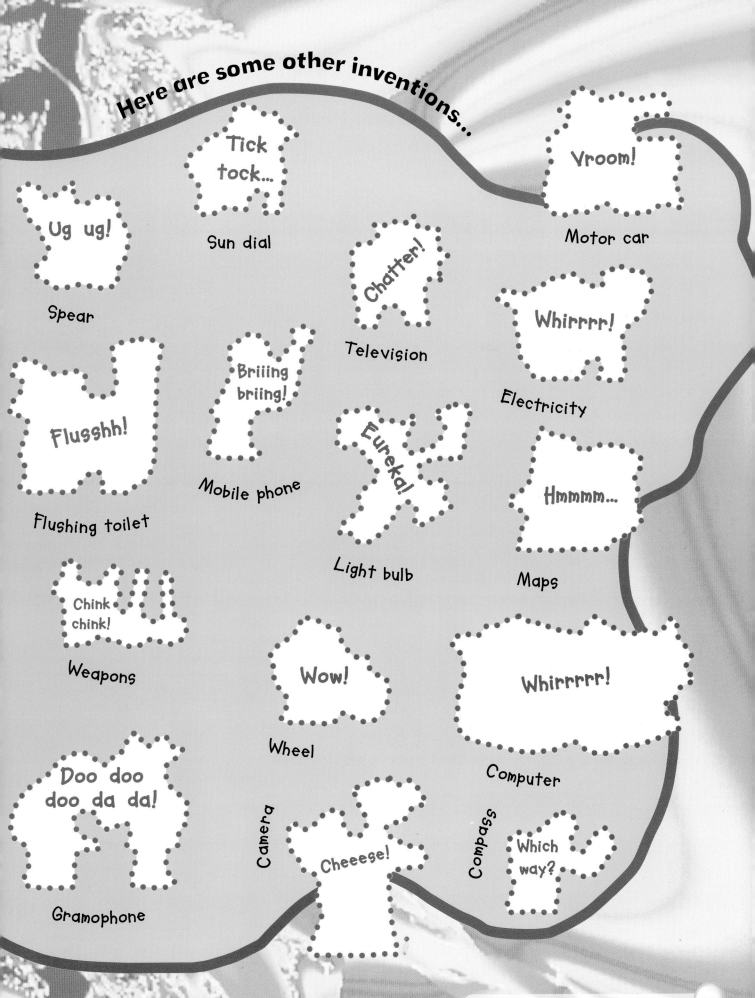

Here are some other inventions...

Tick tock...
Sun dial

Vroom!
Motor car

Ug ug!
Spear

Chatter!
Television

Whirrrr!
Electricity

Flusshh!
Flushing toilet

Briiing briing!
Mobile phone

Eureka!
Light bulb

Hmmm...
Maps

Chink chink!
Weapons

Wow!
Wheel

Whirrrrr!
Computer

Doo doo doo da da!
Gramophone

Camera

Cheeese!

Compass

Which way?

# The first inventors

Complete the scene!

The first inventions were stone tools, made 2.5 million years ago by **Stone Age** people. This meant they could hunt animals for food and make clothes from the skin. They could also carve wood to make musical instruments.

Hunters returning

Gathering wood

Making clothes

Playing a wooden pipe

## Hunting tools

Early hunters were able to kill the biggest animals! We know that they used spears with sharp stone tips to kill animals such as huge woolly mammoths.

Some ancient peoples made their houses from the bones and tusks of mammoths that they hunted.

Stone Age hunters

Mammoths

# Fire

People first made fire more than 250,000 years ago. It gave heat to cook food, and light. Thousands of years later, flint stones were used to make sparks, which could light dried grass and wood.

Add some more cave art!

# Stone Age tool gallery!

Hand axe

Flint axe

Flint scraper

Arrow head

Saw

Find the stickers on page 60  **53**

# How many?

Count how many of each item there are on these pages and write your answers in the boxes.

| Boneshaker | Flint axe | Sandwich | Umbrella | Telescope | Robot | MP3 player | Light bulb |
|---|---|---|---|---|---|---|---|
| 6 | 2 | 5 | 1 | 2 | 4 | 7 | 8 |

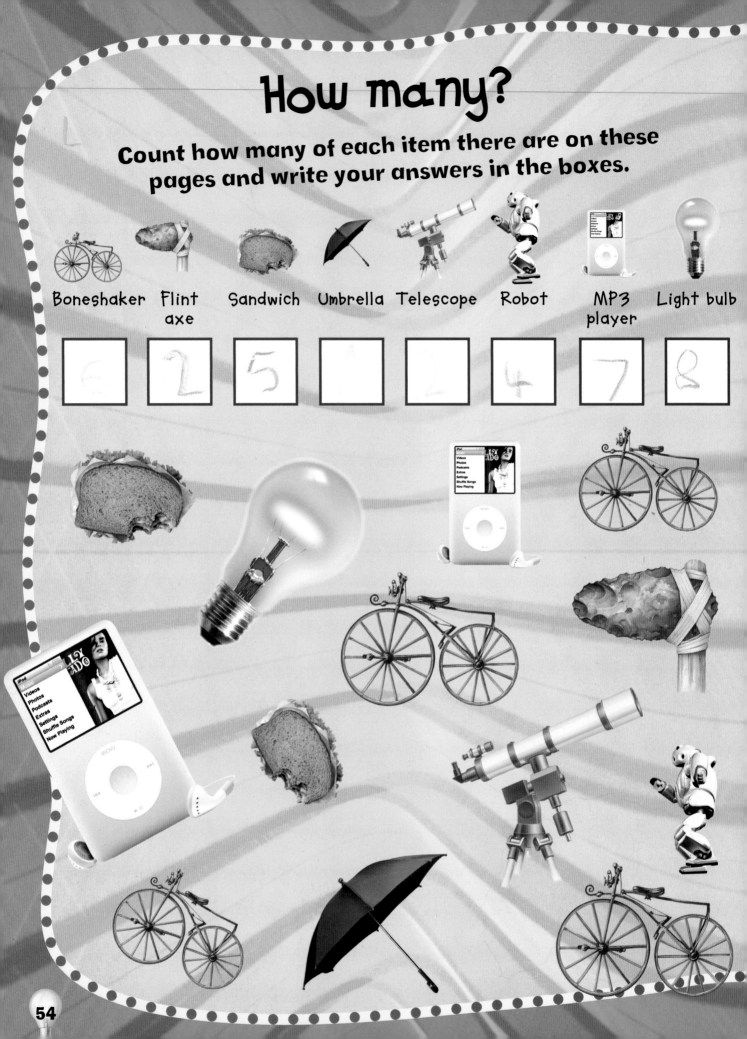

# The wheel

**The people of Mesopotamia (modern Iraq) invented the wheel over 5500 years ago. They made the first wheels by fixing wooden planks together.**

Solid plank wheel

# Spokes

From 1800 BC, the ancient Egyptians used spoked wheels on their fighting chariots. Spoked wheels are much lighter than solid plank wheels.

Egyptian warriors on a chariot

## Bicycle gallery!

Velocopide or 'boneshaker'

Penny farthing

Hobby

Aerodynamic bicycle

Mountain bicycle

Tandem bicycle

## DOT-TO-DOT AND COLOUR

...this monster truck! Monster trucks have huge, rubber tyres. They compete in shows to drive over rows of cars.

**Use these stickers on page 51**

**Stickers for fun – use anywhere you like**

Use these stickers on pages 52, 53, 56 and 65

Use these stickers on pages 66, 67, 68 and 69

**Use these stickers on pages 66, 70 and 71**

**Use these stickers on page 72**

63

# Incredible inventions

Many inventions have shaped our world. One of these is writing, which was first used more than 5000 years ago. Others include the telephone, light bulb, car and aeroplane.

The Sumerians were the first people to write. They used pictures to represent words.

The first written words

The first engine-powered aeroplane was invented by the Wright brothers in 1903.

The **telephone** was invented by Alexander Graham Bell in 1876.

The **light bulb** was invented by Thomas Edison in 1879.

The **motor car** was invented by Karl Benz in 1886.

## Camera corner

It took eight hours to take the first photograph. Frenchman Joseph Nicéphore Niépce was the inventor and the photo was of rooftops. Cameras use lenses to focus an image.

Find the other inventions with lenses!

Polaroid camera

Early camera

Digital camera

Spectacles

Microscope

Telescope

# Everyday inventions

There are lots of inventions that we use every single day, such as toothbrushes, pens and clocks. Life would be very difficult without them!

In 1596 Englishman Sir John Harrington invented the toilet flush.

## In a day...

In just one day we use lots of different inventions. Here are just a few. Can you think of any others?

**Find the missing inventions!**

**Alarm clock**

You get woken up by this in the morning...

**Biro**

You write with this...

**Trainers or 'sneakers'**

You might put these on before you go outside...

**Sandwich**

You eat this at lunchtime...

**Umbrella**

You might use this when it rains...

**Television**

When you get home you might watch this...

# Food and drink

Many kinds of food and drink were invented, some by accident! In 1853, a customer in a New York restaurant complained his chips were too thick. The chef prepared some more and cut them wafer-thin. He ended up inventing crisps, or potato chips.

In the 1860s, sausages in buns were sold from carts on the streets of New York. The bun meant a plate wasn't needed.

Hot dog

**Tea bag**

American Thomas Sullivan invented the tea bag in 1908. The first tea bags were made from silk.

Bubblegum was first invented in the USA by Henry Fleer in 1906. It was called Blibber-Blubber.

Bubblegum

# Kitchen corner

Many inventions can be found in the kitchen. Most heat, cook and store food and drink.

Refrigerator

Kettle

Oven

What is cooking in the microwave?

**Find the stickers on pages 61 and 63** **67**

# Fun inventions

Many inventions are fun and entertaining. Some, such as fireworks and playing cards, were invented many centuries ago.

Roller skates

Teddy bear

Rubik's cube

## Toys

Children have played with toys for thousands of years. The Egyptian king Tutankhamun was found buried with toys in his tomb, and the ancient Greeks and Romans played with dolls and spinning tops.

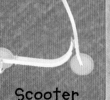

Marbles

Scooter

Spinning top

Find the missing toys!

Rocking horse

Toy car

Yo-yo

Lego®

## Picture puzzle

Gunpowder was invented in China in the 9th century where it was used in fireworks.

# Fun technology

In the 1900s, the first animated films were cartoons. They were made up of many separate hand-drawn images. Today, computers are used to create the images. This is called CGI (computer-generated imagery).

Disney Pixar character Wall·E

Disney's Mickey Mouse

## Gadget gallery!

Mobile phone

Hand-held games console

Portable MP3 player

Satellite navigation system

Laptop computer

**Find the stickers on page 63**

# Can you find...?

 ...An early invention that was made with stone

An invention you can ride that has wheels...

 ...A monster vehicle with huge tyres

The first written words...

 ...A four-wheeled vehicle invented by Karl Benz

A pair of lenses that help you see better...

 ...Something you can eat made with two slices of bread

A disk that can play music...

...A soft bear that you can cuddle

They light up the sky on November 5th...

# ARMS AND ARMOUR

# Arms and armour

**For thousands of years, people have used arms and armour for hunting and in times of war.**

**Arms are weapons such as swords, axes or guns. Armour is protective clothing such as helmets or metal coverings that protect the body during battle.**

**Early armour was made from wood or leather and the first arms were made from wood or stone.**

◀ Knights had the best arms and armour and were the most experienced men in any army.

# Here are some arms, armour and warriors...

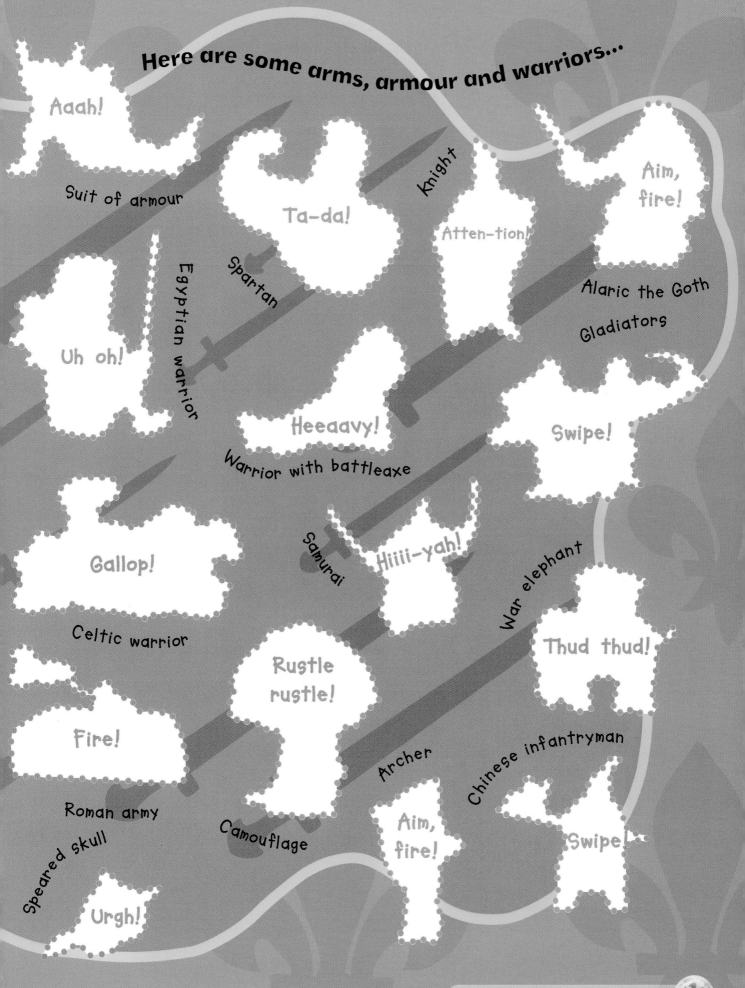

Aaah!

Suit of armour

Ta-da!

Knight

Atten-tion!

Aim, fire!

Alaric the Goth

Uh oh!

Egyptian warrior

Spartan

Gladiators

Heeaavy!

Warrior with battleaxe

Swipe!

Gallop!

Samurai

Hiiii-yah!

War elephant

Celtic warrior

Thud thud!

Rustle rustle!

Fire!

Archer

Chinese infantryman

Roman army

Camouflage

Aim, fire!

Swipe!

Speared skull

Urgh!

**Find the stickers on page 82**

# Arms

Arms are weapons used in battle to attack other people. The first proper weapons were spears made with a stone point on the end of a wooden pole.

Stone Age spear

Dutch godendag spear

Viking spear

English bill spear

## Early arms

Early arms, such as the boomerang and the Maori short club, were made of wood. As metal started to be used more and more, weapons such as spears, swords and axes, were made.

Find the missing weapons!

The earliest-known spears are 400,000 years old and were found in Germany.

Boomerang

Maori short club

Knife

Egyptian war axe

Spiked club

Bow and arrows

## Early warfare

At the battle of Lechfeld in AD 955, the Germans and Magyars (Hungarians) fought with spears, swords and bows and arrows.

# Later arms

As technology developed, so did weapons. They were now able to fire bullets. The first guns were not very powerful and could not shoot a bullet with much force.

## Blunderbuss

Guards on horse-drawn coaches carried heavy blunderbusses to protect their passengers.

## Early pistol

This early pistol, called a wheel-lock pistol, was the first reliable firing weapon.

## 'Brown bess'

In the 1740s, British soldiers carried a gun called a 'Brown Bess'. A long dagger called a bayonet could be fitted to the end.

# Sword gallery!

Indian talwar sword

Samurai sword

Gladius

Viking long sword

Double-edged sword

Gladiator training sword

**Find the stickers on page 84**

# How many?

Count how many of each item there are on these pages and write your answers in the boxes.

Samurai    Trebuchet    Gladiator training sword    Boomerang    Viking iron helmet    Indian shield    Roman armour    Native North American

# Armour

Armour is worn by warriors to protect them. It was also worn by animals such as horses and war elephants.

By 1300 knights were dressing their horses in armour to protect them in battle.

Knight and horse in chainmail

## Chainmail

Early knights wore a type of armour called chainmail. It was made of lots of tiny iron rings linked together.

# Armour gallery!

War elephant

Gauntlet

Russian armour

Chainmail

Medieval breastplate

Roman armour

## DOT-TO-DOT AND COLOUR

...this knight in a suit of armour! By the 1400s, plate armour like this covered the knight's entire body.

**Use these stickers on page 75**

**Stickers for fun – use anywhere you like**

Use these stickers on pages 77, 80 and 89

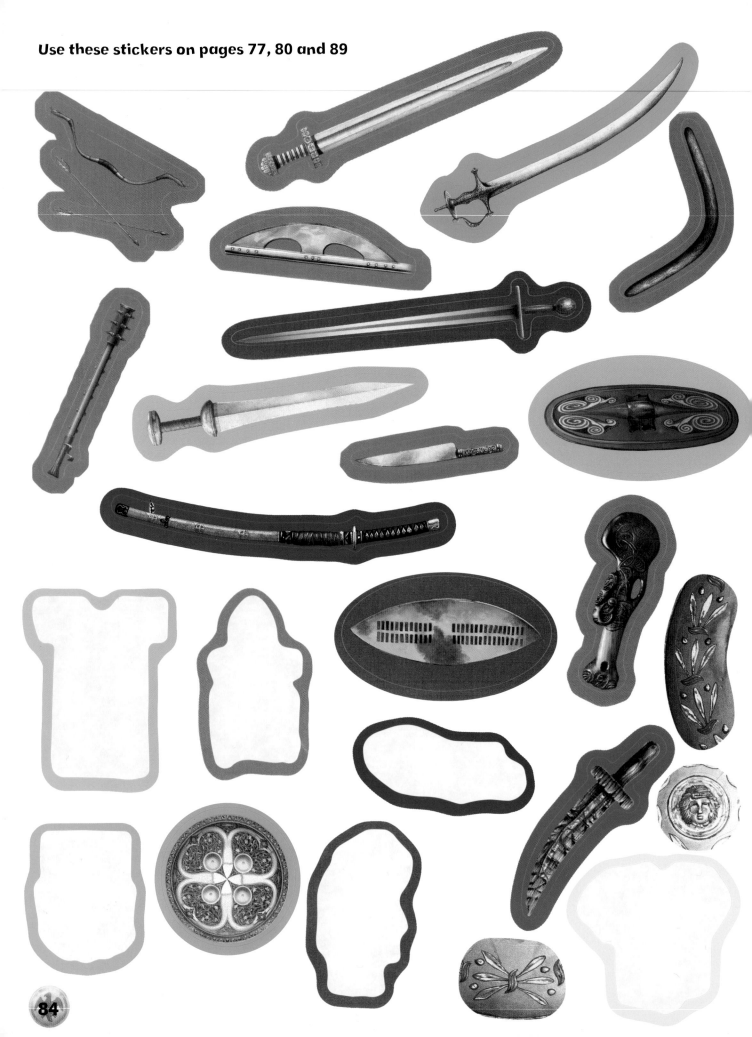

84

**Use these stickers on pages 93, 94 and 95**

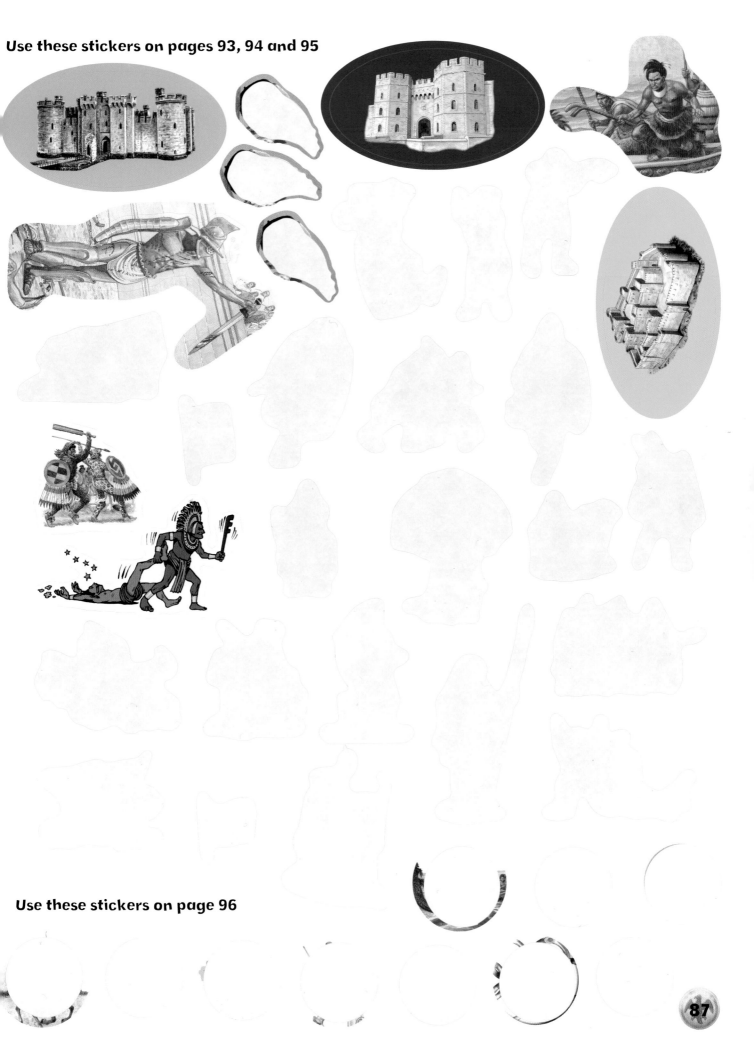

**Use these stickers on page 96**

# Helmets and shields

As well as body armour, warriors wore helmets and carried shields for extra protection in battle. Helmets were made of metal and shields were made from metal, wood or leather.

Gladiators wore helmets decorated with plumes of coloured feathers or horsehair. This made them look bigger in battle.

Viking helmet

Gladiator helmet

Sutton Hoo helmet

Knight's bascinet helmet

Greek helmet

# Shield corner

Shields were decorated with bright colours and patterns to look more impressive in battle. Gladiator shields were carved with images of gods and decorated with gold to impress the audience.

Decorate the gladiator shield!

Indian shield

Celtic shield

Zulu shield

Find the stickers on page 84 **89**

# Warriors

Throughout history, brave soldiers called warriors have fought in terrible wars. They used many different kinds of arms and armour.

In battle, Aztec warriors would dress as fierce animals such as eagles and jaguars.

## Around the world

Warriors from different parts of the world had their own kind of weapons, shields and armour.

Find the missing warriors!

Zulu warrior of Africa

Shang warrior of China

Indian soldier

Native warrior of North America

Samurai warrior of Japan

Aztec warrior of South America

## Greeks

Greek soldiers were called hoplites. This meant 'armoured men'. They fought with a shield, helmet, spear and sword.

Hoplite

## Romans

The Roman army was made up of legions – groups of about 6000 men. A legionary was a paid, professional soldier.

Legionary

# Barbarians

During Roman times, people who lived outside the Roman empire were called Barbarians.

Barbarians got their name because people thought their foreign language sounded like they were saying "bar bar".

Dacian warrior

Dacian warriors from Romania were armed with a sharp, curved sword

Hun

Huns from Asia fought on horseback with bows and spears, without armour

# Knights

The first knights wore chainmail and later they wore plate armour. Knights fought on horseback, and on foot in hand-to-hand combat.

Knights

# Gladiator gallery!

Andabatae

Velite

Paeginiarius

Dimachaerus

Secutor

Hoplomachus

Find the stickers on page 85

# Into battle

**A lot of preparation was needed for battle. Warriors had to be trained and armed with weapons. Sometimes armies travelled long distances to fight.**

Zulu warriors wore ostrich and crane feathers on their helmets.

## Zulu army

Young boys follow the Zulu warriors, carrying bedding, food and spare weapons. A Zulu army began a battle by throwing long spears. Then they would attack with short, stabbing spears.

Zulu army

Greek army

Find the missing shields!

## Greek army

When going into battle, Greek hoplites stood shoulder to shoulder so that their shields overlapped. They pointed their spears forwards over the shields.

## Picture puzzle

In battle, Roman soldiers stood close together and overlapping their shields. This was called the 'tortoise' formation.

# Gladiator fights

Fights took place in an arena (a large open space surrounded by seating). Not every fight ended in death – if a gladiator fought well he was allowed to live.

Gladiator fight

**Find the missing warriors!**

Polynesian war canoe

## Island wars

A Polynesian war canoe on its way to a raid on another island. The warriors paddling the canoe kept their weapons close beside them.

# Castle corner

When an army attacked a castle it often used a weapon called a trebuchet. This was like a giant catapult that could hurl heavy stones or burning objects towards the castle walls.

**What is the trebuchet hurling?**

Windsor Castle, England

Krak des Chevaliers, Syria

Bodium Castle, England

**Find the stickers on pages 85 and 87**

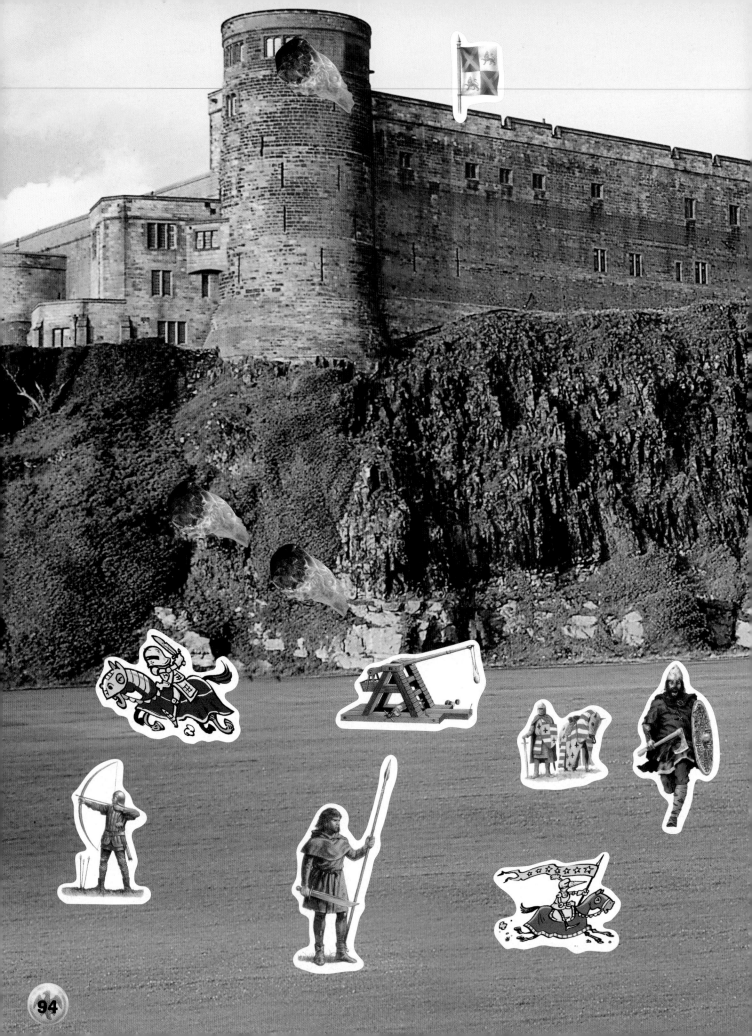

**Find the stickers on page 87**

# Can you find...?

 ...A Maori club made of wood

A sword a gladiator-in-training used...

 ...A close-up of chainmail armour

Armour a Roman warrior would have worn...

 ...The ancient Sutton Hoo helmet

An Indian shield...

 ...A Greek hoplite

A Barbarian on horseback...

 ...A Polynesian war canoe

A fort that might have been under siege...